The Vamp

A Play in one act from the Japanese Legend of the Nabeshima cat

Gerard Van Etten

Alpha Editions

This edition published in 2024

ISBN : 9789362921987

Design and Setting By
Alpha Editions
www.alphaedis.com
Email - info@alphaedis.com

Contents

CAST OF CHARACTERS

PRINCE HIZEN, LORD OF NABESHIMA
BUZEN, HIS CHIEF COUNCILLOR
RUITEN, A PRIEST
ITO SODA, A COMMON SOLDIER
KASHIKU, A MAID
O TOYO, WIFE OF THE PRINCE

TIME: Medieval Japan.

SCENE: The room of O Toyo in the palace.

TIME OF ACTION: Between 10 and 12 p.m.

NOTE.—According to the old Japanese legend, the soul of a cat can enter a human being.

THE VAMPIRE CAT

SCENE. *At R. is a dressing table, upon it a steel mirror, toilet articles, and two lighted candles with ornate shades. R. U. a section of shoji leads to another room, this section is now closed. At R. C. a large section of shoji is open, giving a view of the garden. To the R. of this entrance is a small shrine and Buddha. At L. of the room is a sleeping mat and head rest. By the head rest a lantern, now unlighted. Down L. is an open section of shoji leading to the* PRINCE'S *apartments. Just above it stands a screen. As the curtain rises the* PRINCE *is standing R. C. looking out into the garden.* RUITEN *is down R. and* BUZEN *slightly above him.* BUZEN *crosses L.*

PRINCE. [*Comes down between* RUITEN *and* BUZEN.]
Settle for me tonight
My sicknesses and my fears—
[*To* BUZEN.]   Settle them for me,
Sir Buzen, councillor crafty.
[*To* RUITEN.]   Settle them for me,
Priest Ruiten, the prayerful.

RUITEN.   So are we trying in all ways
Thy pain to relieve
Yet nought seems availing.

PRINCE.   Wracked is my body
With tortures unending
Born of the dreams
That are surging forever
Backward and forward
Thru my brain, weary.

BUZEN.   [*Indicating door L.*]   Around thy bed each night
Have I placed thy samurai
In number one hundred
To guard thy sleep—

RUITEN.   Zealously have I prayed
In the temple called "Miyo In,
"And during the night hours

Have knelt at thy house shrine
Praying to Buddha, the lord of the world.

PRINCE. Yet have I not slept
Entirely untortured.
Slow are thy prayers
In fruit bearing.

RUITEN. Slow because contending with evil—
[*Approaches Prince.*]
With evil in form strange and subtle.
Over this house hangs a spirit
Ne'er resting and ready always for dire deeds.

PRINCE. Such a spirit there must be—but what?

RUITEN. Evil takes many forms but the form of a cat
Is favored by many devils.

PRINCE. [*Startled, the others watch him closely.*] A cat—aye,
truly
And if a cat stalked here
That evil thing must we kill.

RUITEN. Yet such is their power malignant
That they take other forms than the forms of cats—
Even human forms.

PRINCE. Ha!—And the spirit that visits me?
Mayhap that—
Only twice hath it failed of its visit.

BUZEN. And those lost visits, when?

PRINCE. The last two nights.

BUZEN. [*Swelling with pride.*] Then, oh Prince, the cure may
be found.
Better than prayers is the cure   [*Eyeing RUITEN.*]
For prayers have not ears—have not eyes—
Have not weapons—better than prayers is it.

PRINCE. Tell me this cure. It is grudged, Sir Priest?

RUITEN. [*Bowing.*] A cure for my lord could not be grudged.

PRINCE. Well spoken. Say on, Sir Buzen.

BUZEN. First I must beg clemency
For thy hundred samurai
For faithful they are to the bone, yet—

PRINCE. Yet? Why clemency? For what?

BUZEN. On guard, they slept.

PRINCE. Slept?

BUZEN. Aye. Soundly as though deep in saki.

PRINCE. And none roused?

BUZEN. They were as dead
From shortly after the hour of ten
Until dawning.
Awakening they knew they had slept
Yet knew not when the poppy was thrown in their eyes.
Even as one man none knew
And were deep amazed and full of shame.
Each night it was the same.

PRINCE. [*Angrily.*] So, they slept.
While I, on my couch,
Through the hours writhed—
Writhed and twisted—
Weakening ever—
Not sleep, yet dreaming—
Oh, horrible dreams.

RUITEN. Of what were these horrible dreams?
What was their substance?

PRINCE. [*Mystified at the memory.*] There would come a soft stealing—
As of draperies hushed and lifted
For silence in walking;

Like soft, silken draperies
Wrapped about stealthy limbs.
Then a shape clothed for sleep
As women are clothed—
Sinuous and vague in movement,
Then taking form slowly—
The form—a lie!—a lie!   [*Covers his face and goes upstage.*]

RUITEN.   The form?

PRINCE.   [*Turns.*]   O Toyo!

RUITEN. BUZEN.   [*Rubbing their hands.*]   Ah!

PRINCE.   [*Comes down R.,* RUITEN *and* BUZEN *are together a little L.*]
Came she to me—
Leaned o'er me—
Caressed me
Yet soothed not.
Her lips to mine—
Her lips but not sweet.
Then here on my throat
Would she place them
And all my life seemed to smother—
Out of me flowed the life-blood
In a deep stream
Like a tide
Forced by the gods,
Against its will,
To flow far away and yet farther.

BUZEN.   So does a vampire
Sucking her victim
Draw from him
His blood and his marrow.

PRINCE.   Guard thy words!—As my strength ebbed
She drew back
Red-lipped and smiling,

Smiling and laughing
Though her laughter was silent.
Then with a final shimmer
Of silent silks she vanished—
So was it done.

RUITEN. So always the dream?
If dream it were.

PRINCE. The dream—
I think yet it was a dream—
So was it always.

BUZEN. But the last two nights?

PRINCE. Came she as usual
Flowing over the floor
Like a spectre enrobed
And beautified.
But as she bent o'er me
She paused as if startled
And, slowly gazing about,
Turned and was gone.
Last night she paused
As if speaking to someone
Though I could see no one.

BUZEN. But the cause of her turning?

RUITEN. Turned she startled—
Turned she slowly—
Turned she wonderingly?

PRINCE. Slowly, as if she felt
A strange presence.

RUITEN. Feared she?

PRINCE. She left me.

BUZEN. But trembling or calm?

PRINCE. Calmly, as from a thing hated
And more powerful than she
Whom she would not rouse to action.

BUZEN. [*Rubbing his hands.*] Good.

PRINCE. What is good?

BUZEN. That which thou speakest of.

PRINCE. How so?

BUZEN. [*Comes forward towards the Prince.*] It proves that I
have humbly succeeded—
[*Grudgingly.*] Through the help of another, 'tis true—
But yet succeeded in bringing my lord honorable help.

RUITEN. Indeed it is so.

PRINCE. Say on, very wise councillor.

BUZEN. [*Puffing up.*] Without more words than are fit
This then is the way of the cure.
When long had thine illness ravaged and worn thee
And many nights had you tossed by weird visions enthralled,
No cures affecting, no prayers availing thee [*Glances at*
RUITEN.]
Then councilled I with thy wise ones—
And, too, with Priest Ruiten—

RUITEN. I, you should name first,
For without my prayers your wisdom was nought.

BUZEN. To continue briefly.
All our heads together brought no solution—

PRINCE. True, true.

BUZEN. [*Bowing.*] Humbly I acknowledge my head
Empty and brainless.
Yet even from idiots lips
Wisdom oft falls unexpected
And therefore more wonderful.

Now it is told in old tales
Of how Iyaiyasu met—

RUITEN.   Short, abrupt is thy tale.

PRINCE.   The cure, Sir Buzen,
The hour passes.

BUZEN.   [*Bowing.*]   I crave honorable leniency.
To be brief—

PRINCE.   Aye, brief.

BUZEN.   Discouraged and sick at heart
At the sufferings of my great lord,
I was retiring to my room
By way of the garden
And the hour was the Hour of the Fox.
I heard a splashing in the pool
And drawing near
Saw a young soldier washing.
I spoke to him asking,
"Who art thou?"
"Retainer to my Lord Nabeshima,
Prince of Hizen," he answered.
Then talked I with him. Of thy sickness
We talked. And he was ashamed of thy samurai's sleeping.
He begged to be allowed to guard thy sleep
Also for, being a common soldier, it was not permitted.
So earnestly talked he that I promised to consult
With the other councillors and see what could be done.
"So tell me your name, young sir," I said.
"Ito Soda is my name, honorable sir,
And for your kind words I thank you.
"So I consulted and the result was
We granted his request.

PRINCE.   And he, too, has watched the two nights past?

RUITEN.   Aye, and he slept not
Though the samurai were heavy with sleep-fumes.

BUZEN. I will tell.

RUITEN. [*Elbows* BUZEN *out of the way and comes forward.*] You are honorably hoarse.
He slept not, as I say—

PRINCE. How kept he awake?
Since many slept spell-bound
How broke he the spell?

RUITEN. With him he brought
Oiled paper and laid it
Down on the matting
Sitting upon it.
When o'er his eyes sleep stole
And wearily weighted them
He drew out his sharp dirk
And in his thigh thrust it
By pain driving the poppy fumes off.
Ever and again he twisted
The dirk in the raw wound
And the thick blood-drops
Soiled not the matting
Because of the oiled paper.

PRINCE. Indeed this is no common soldier,
This Ito Soda.

BUZEN. Indeed not—

RUITEN. To continue—[*Retires upstage, disgruntled.*]

BUZEN. [*Pushing forward.*] As I was saying, oh Prince,
His eyes never closed.
During the Reign of the Rat
He heard, in this room, O Toyo
Tossing and moaning
As if in great fear of something
She could not escape from.
Even at the same moment
As the beginnings of her moanings

Came a cat-call from the garden—
Then nearer—then ghostly paddings
As of padded claws on matting,
And an evil presence seemed hovering
And lurking near in the darkness.
O Toyo gave a low scream—than all was silence.
Soon she came stealthily
Through the shoji—cat-like her step—
Glassy her eyes—Claw-like her hands—
Bent she over you with curled lips—
Then she turned, even as you have said,
And, seeing a waking watcher,
Left as she came.

RUITEN. [*Comes down.*]   The second night of Ito Soda's watching
She threatened him in low words
But he made as to stab her
And she melted before him
Laughing a little.
And he heard the rustle of her garments
As she regained this room
Though he saw not her passage hither.

PRINCE.   Thicker with each word the horror about me.[*Turns away to R.*]   Doubts to beliefs—beliefs to actions—Love unto hate. [*Turns to them almost pleadingly.*]Tell me it is not O Toyo.

BUZEN.   I questioned her maid, Kashiku,
And found that O Toyo's couch
Was empty even at the time
Of the weird visit to thee.

PRINCE. [*Overwhelmed.*]   So, it was O Toyo!
In the soul of a flower, a demon—
On the sweet lips, poison.

BUZEN.   There is only one course—

RUITEN.   The one road—

PRINCE. And I take it!

BUZEN. [*Moves toward door L.*] The samurai are gathered.

PRINCE. Summon Ito Soda. [BUZEN *exits L.*]

RUITEN. Hard is the fate of man
Here on this dark earth.
Many the shapes and the shadows
Stalking abroad.
Yet ever the gentle Buddha
From the Lotus Fields watches
And guards every life that lives.

PRINCE. [*Puts one hand on* RUITEN'S *shoulder.*] Priest, have
not many
Vampires bleeding them
And dream it is another thing?

RUITEN. The soul is often a vampire to the body.

PRINCE. And that evil thing must we kill.

ITO SODA. [*Enters L., kneels before the* PRINCE. RUITEN *takes
up R. a little and* BUZEN *re-entering after* ITO SODA *goes up
C.*]Honorable Prince, humbly I answer thy summons.

PRINCE. Rise, Ito Soda.
Faithful beyond words art thou,
This know I as all hath been told me.
No longer call thyself a common soldier
But a samurai of the Prince of Hizen.
And the two swords will I give thee on the morrow.

ITO SODA. On my knees I humbly thank thee. [*Rises.*]

PRINCE. Now time presses.
O Toyo will be coming
In from the garden.
As usual shall the hundred sleepy samurai
Guard my couch. Let Ito Soda
Remain here hidden and watchful.

When O Toyo rises to enter my chamber—
Your dirk is sharp, Ito Soda?

ITO SODA.   [*Draws dirk.*]   As a moonbeam on a cold night.

PRINCE.   And you know how to use it.

ITO SODA.   I will place this screen, thus.
[*Goes to screen L. and opens it so as to form a hiding place between the sleeping mat and the door L.*]
So will I wait the moment.

PRINCE. So be it. It is a good plan
And on the one road. Let us about it.   [*Exits L. followed by* BUZEN *and* RUITEN. ITO SODA *goes behind the screen.* O TOYO *is heard singing in the garden.*]

O TOYO.   [*Outside.*]   Moonlit convulvus
Through the night hours
Wan are their faces
Ghostly sweet.

Richer by daylight
Drinking of sunshine
As thirsty souls drink
At a shrine.

Fair are the faces
Glassed in the quiet pools
Maidens low-bending
Vain ones.

[*The singing stops abruptly.*]   Kashiku, is not that a cat
Stealing stealthily there?
She snarls—quick—[O TOYO *enters B. C. quickly and very frightened, turns and looks back, hurries* KASHIKU *in.* KASHIKU *follows much less disturbed at any fear of a cat than over her mistress' fright.*]

KASHIKU.   [*Shuts the shoji R. C. and comes to* O TOYO.]   You are all atremble.

O TOYO.   Quick, let me be safe in slumber.   [*Crosses to dressing table.*]

KASHIKU.   [*Follows her and attends to her hair while* O TOYO *kneels before the glass.*]   Several nights lately have I heard my lady moaning
As though even in sleep were she troubled.
The worry over your honorable lord hath disturbed thee.

O TOYO.   Your ears are over keen.
I am happy when I sleep.
How can I moan, being happy?
You are dull.

KASHIKU.   Perhaps it was the wind or the echo of my lord's moaning.

O TOYO.   Moaning or was it singing?
I would it were singing
For singing is sweeter
On the lips of those dying.

KASHIKU.   Dying?

O TOYO.   When those whom we love are passing—
Even under our hands are passing—
And our love weans them from life
And our kisses suck out the blood-life,
Then would we touch them no more,
Then would we kiss them no more,
But a power greater than we
And a power that we fear
Forces us on in our love-killing.

KASHIKU.   There is in your voice a vibration, as even the winds in the pine-tops
When, in the autumn, they echo the summer's death-song;
There is in your eyes a strange light as if the soul of another
Looked out from your curtaining lashes and dimmed the sweet light there abiding.

Oh, mistress, surely you are different than what you once were.

O Toyo. [*Crosses C. slowly.*] Even now comes the hour and the struggle
And I do the bidding of that which is in me.
How I hate the feel of his flesh
Quivering under my lips
And the loathsome taste of the blood-drops
Thick on my lips that would soothe him and cannot.

Kashiku. Can anything soothe more than thy lips,
More than the lips that love him?
I cannot understand the words of your saying.
You are happy and tearful all in a moment,
Your soul seems a sky full of sunshine and clouds.
[*Coming to her.*] Even now as my hand touches you, you are trembling.
Is it the cat that crept upon us
Whose shape still affrights you?

O Toyo. Thou hast said it—My soul is as thou sayest.
My dreams are sweet and again bitter.
Once came a dream horrible above all dreams.

Kashiku. What dream, my lady?

O Toyo. The night when you found me there on the floor.Do you remember?

Kashiku. Well. You were all distraught and the bosom of your gown
Was torn open and you clutched your throat
As if you were wounded there.
But there was no mark.
And you let wild words fall from your lips
And none knew their meaning.

O Toyo. The Prince and I walked in the garden
And there at the shoji I left him.
As I entered

There entered
With me a spirit
And its breath fell upon me—
Dumb my tongue in my mouth
And frozen my marrow.
Suddenly it leapt upon me
And as I fell downward
Flashed the spirit into mine eyes—
A cat, two-tailed and hairy—
And it's teeth sank in my throat here—
Can you see a mark?   [*Exposes her throat to* KASHIKU.]

KASHIKU.   The skin is as smooth as satin and perfect.

O TOYO.   Then came darkness upon me—and so you found
me.
So strong is the dream within me
I wonder if it be a dream or no.

KASHIKU.   You had walked that evening in the garden.

O TOYO.   I had rather dreamed I walked—say I dreamed it.

KASHIKU.   The Prince was with—

O TOYO.   Yet it was a dream, question it not.
I would go to rest peacefully.
He, too, shall rest peacefully—
I shall not kiss my lord tonight.   [*Crosses L.*]

KASHIKU.   Not kiss him?

O TOYO.   I think not I shall kiss him.
I would not pain his slumbers—
He has paled so and his face is so thin.
In the night he lies like a strong flower
And a strange flower, bled of its life—
Like a strong flower weakened.
And at its sight my dreams are bitter.
But as I gaze a change comes over all things
And I hold in my hands a beautiful flower

Which I kiss with my lips
Holding my lips long to it,
Draining its sweetness.
And a cloud passes over
And on my lips are clots of blood!

KASHIKU.   Such dreamings are not good.
I find the silken coverlets tossed in the morning,
Twisted and thrown about as if you slept ill.

O TOYO.   It is not O Toyo who tosses them—
It is the dream O Toyo.

KASHIKU.   Two nights lately have I imagined you called to
me
But entering you were not here—but there with your lord
soothing his sufferings.

O TOYO.   Drinking at strange fountains and unknown
springs—Drinking of sacred waters sacred to unknown gods.
And as I drink another life becomes my life
And he is mine—utterly mine, at last!

KASHIKU.   You frighten me—

O TOYO.   Be not frightened—you have no need.
Now I shall sleep.
He, too, is sleeping. Perhaps—perhaps he is suffering.
Shall I touch him with my hands?
Perhaps he is hungry for my kisses—Shall I kiss him?

KASHIKU.   It were a fitting thing to kiss thy lord.

O TOYO.   You know not what you say, Kashiku.

KASHIKU.   My lady—

O TOYO.   You have not heard me say strange things,
Kashiku.

KASHIKU.   I have heard—

O TOYO.   Nothing.

KASHIKU.   Nothing, my lady.

O TOYO.   Put out the lamps.   [KASHIKU *blows out candles on dressing table.*]
Go now, Kashiku, and do you sleep deeply,
Breathing poppies.

KASHIKU.   My lady—

O TOYO.   Go.   [KASHIKU *opens shoji R. and goes out shutting it after her. O* TOYO *crosses, too, and lies on the sleeping mat. The room is almost in total darkness.*]

O TOYO.   I shall kiss him—I shall kiss him!   [*The lantern at the head of the sleeping mat glows more and more brightly until a cat's head appears on it. At this moment a cat-call comes from the garden.* (NOTE.—If these effects cannot be gotten with no hint of the ludicrous, have the lantern glow with increasing light but use no cat's head or cat call.) *With the increase of light, O* TOYO *has begun to moan and toss and at the moment of the cat-call she rises as in a trance and goes towards the door L. As she passes the screen* ITO SODA *steps out from behind it and plunges his dirk into her back; she falls with a little, stifled cry. Instantly, in utter darkness, the curtain falls.*]

END OF THE PLAY.

Milton Keynes UK
Ingram Content Group UK Ltd.
UKHW030744071024
449371UK00006B/561

9 789362 921987